Adventures of the Unde...

R-R-RESPECT

Story by University of Florida Record-SettingFootball Player, *Mr. Wayne Fields*

Written and Illustrated by Jenny Dearinger

Dedication by Wayne Fields

To My Parents,
the Lights of My Life.

Jerry Miller, my step-father
Geraldine Miller, my mother
And
Dr. Julius Gazelle Fields, my biological father

Ricky the Shark, Preston the Octopus, and Donald the Whale, met the new guy in the bay. Wayne the Dolphin was shy and had a stutter.

The boys joked around until the dolphin started coming out of his shell.

"Let's pl-pl-play a game," Wayne stuttered.

"Great," said Preston. "Let's play paddleball."

"N-n-no," said Wayne.

"Let's play shellball," said Ricky.

"N-n-no," said Wayne.

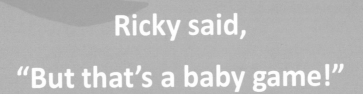

Ricky said,
"But that's a baby game!"

Ricky looked at Preston. Preston looked at Donald. Donald looked at Ricky.

The three boys did not like Wayne's choice. But they politely played tiddly-stars.

"Who's going first," asked Ricky.

"I will! It's *MY* game!," said Wayne.

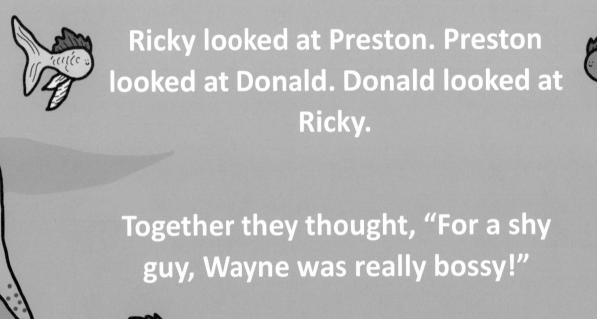

Ricky looked at Preston. Preston looked at Donald. Donald looked at Ricky.

Together they thought, "For a shy guy, Wayne was really bossy!"

"Let's go get saltwater taffy," said Wayne when the game was finished.

"Okay," said the others.

When they got to the taffy shop, Wayne told the shop keeper, "I'll have a choc-choc-chocolate taffy and so will my fr-fr-friends."

"But I wanted strawberry," said Ricky.
"And I wanted vanilla," said Preston.
"And I wanted mint," said Donald.

Wayne would not listen to the three boys.

The next day, Wayne searched for Ricky, Preston, and Donald. He found them behind a sunken ship playing tailball.

"Hey guys, let's play sn-sn-snail spoons and then have a worm cracker sn-sn-snack," said Wayne.

The boys looked down.
Ricky shuffled his tail.
Preston covered his face with his arm.
Donald said, "We don't want to play with you. We wanted to be your friend, but you don't care about our feelings."

Wayne swam away all alone.

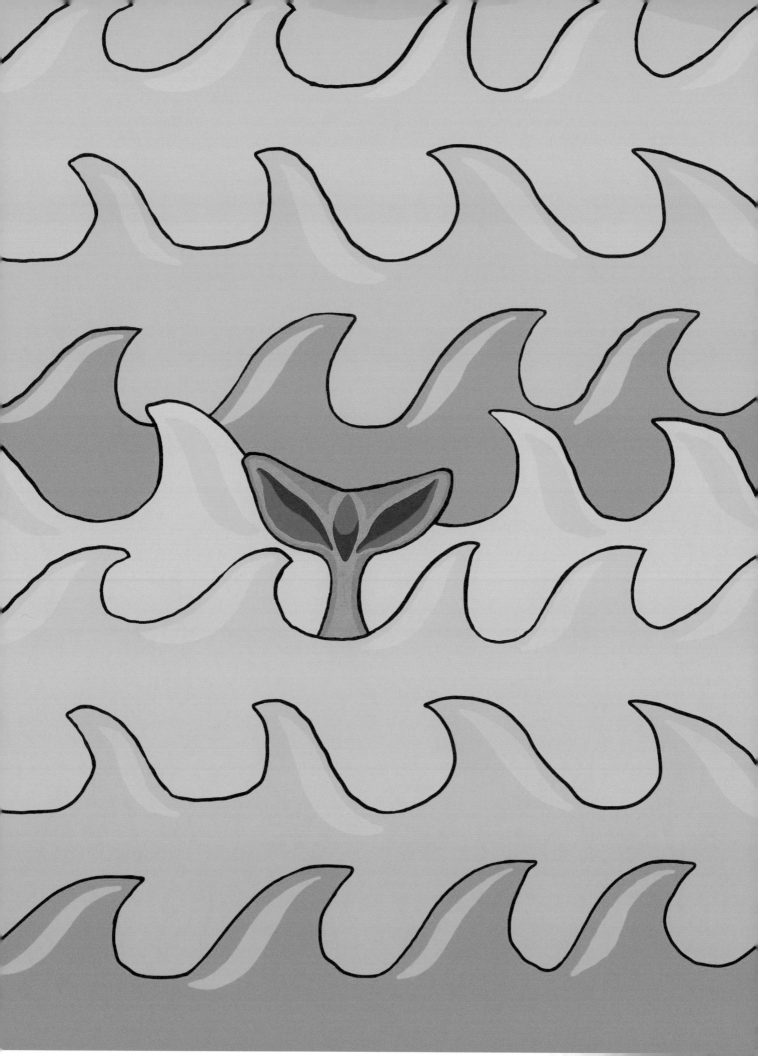

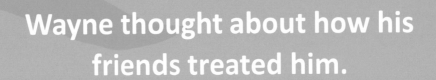

Wayne thought about how his
friends treated him.

They let him pick the game,

and be first,

and let him choose the saltwater
taffy.

They didn't care about his
stutter. They were good friends.

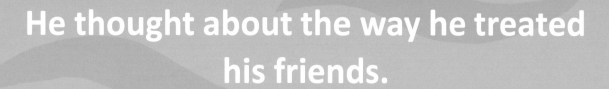

He thought about the way he treated his friends.

He didn't make a good choice and chose a game nobody else wanted to play.

He wasn't a good sport and wanted to be first.

He didn't listen and picked the taffy.

No wonder they didn't want to play with him!

Wayne thought.

And thought some more.

Wayne knew exactly what he should do for his friends!

The next day, Wayne found the other boys hiding in the same place in the bay.

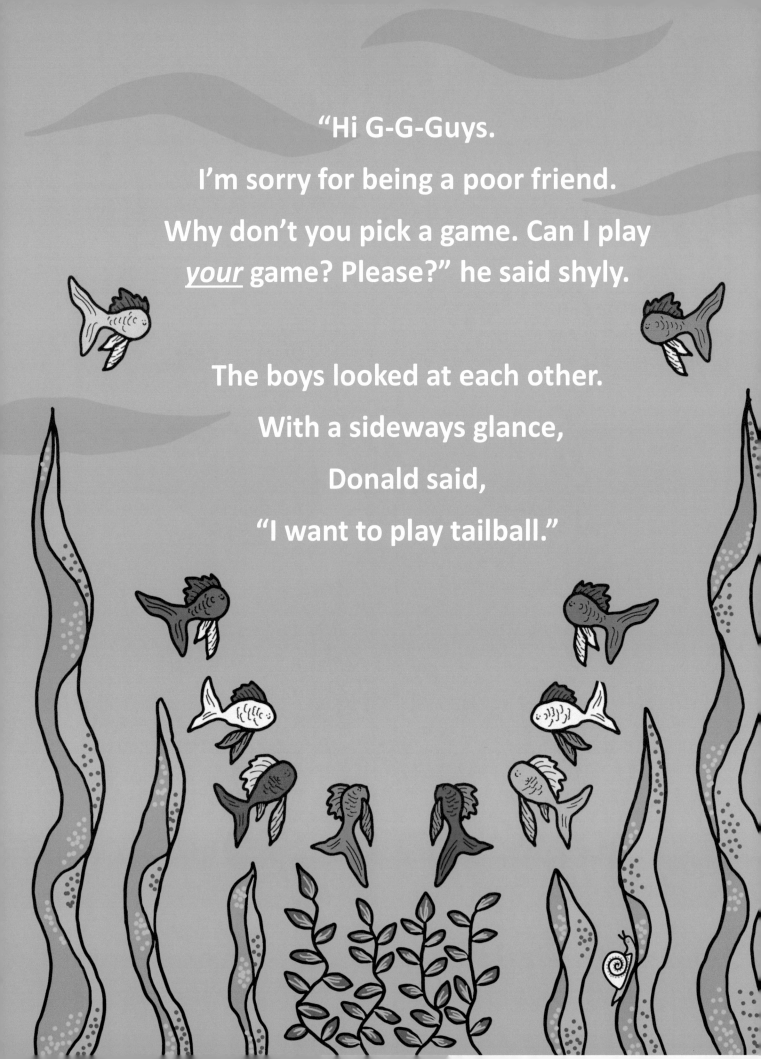

"Hi G-G-Guys.

I'm sorry for being a poor friend.

Why don't you pick a game. Can I play _your_ game? Please?" he said shyly.

The boys looked at each other.

With a sideways glance,

Donald said,

"I want to play tailball."

With a happy smile,
Wayne said, "Yes! That's a good choice. Let's play
Donald's game."
"Who's going to go first," asked Ricky.
"I want to go first," said Donald.
Wayne clapped.

After the game, Preston said, "Let's go get a snack."

All four friends went to the saltwater taffy store and got the flavor they wanted.

Ricky said, "Wayne, you make good choices. You can pick the game next time."

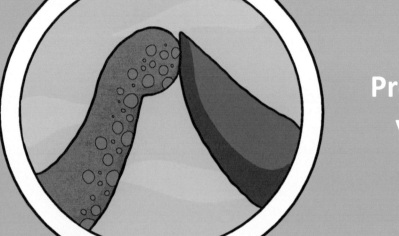

Preston said, "Wayne, you're a good sport. You can play first."

Donald said, "Wayne, you're a good listener. You can help us decide what to get next time we go to the taffy store."

Thank you for listening.

Wayne said,
"I I-I-learned that making
Good Choices,
Being a Good Sport,
and
I-I-*Listening*
are part of being a good
friend.

When you give

R-R-RESPECT

You get

Respect Back!"

A Little About Mr. Fields and Football Life Lessons

Mr. Fields loved all sports from an early age, but football was his passion! Mr. Fields played for the University of Florida in 1972, 1973, and 1974. He holds the record for the number of interceptions during those years. Mr. Fields was also drafted by the Pittsburg Steelers.

While the game is fun and meaningful, the life lessons Mr. Fields learned from Playing football have become a part of his everyday life.

One of the main lessons Mr. Fields learned through football is how to treat others with RESPECT.

RESPECT is treating others like their feelings are important and you are listening to what they are saying.

RESPECT is also a LEADERSHIP Quality. Good leaders care about the people around them. Leaders show they care by listening and taking other people's feeling seriously.

When you treat other people like they are important, you become important to them. They will listen to you and RESPECT you in return!

Please, Thank You, and I'm Sorry

Did you know that saying Please, Thank You, and I'm Sorry are not only polite but they are also showing respect?

- How would you feel if someone was bossy and rude to you?

- What words would you use to tell them your feelings were hurt?

- How do you think others feel if you are bossy and rude to them?

- Do you think that other people have more respect for you when you take responsibility for your behavior?

- What are three things you can say to show people you Respect them?

Let's pretend-

- You accidently knock over your drink on someone's paper. What would you do? What would you say?

- You want something. How should you ask for it?

- Someone gives you a present. What should you say?

Everyone is Unique!

Wayne the Dolphin has a stutter, just like the *real* Wayne Fields did when he was young. When Wayne talks sometimes he says the first sound of a word more than once. But that doesn't keep him from being a good friend. He learns to Respect his friends and they learn to Respect him.

Supplies

- Paper
- Crayons
- 3 People
- Imagination

Directions

- With the crayons, on a piece of paper
- Person One draws a head
- Person Two draws a body
- Person Three draws arms and legs
- The three of you have now drawn a Unique Person!
- Think about what makes your person special.
- Think about how this Unique person could be your new friend!
- Do their differences really matter?
- How can you respect their differences?

You can also do this Activity by yourself!

Other Books by Jenny Dearinger

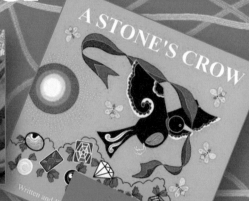

A STONE'S CROW

Written and Illustrated by

FIREBALL TENNIS

Written by
Jenifer Peters Dearinger and Tracey Begley
Illustrated by

PREPOSTEROUS PUMPKINS

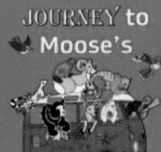

JOURNEY to Moose's

Written and Illustrated by
Jenifer Peters Dearinger

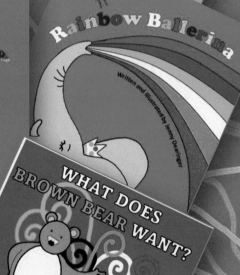

Rainbow Ballerina

Written and Illustrated by Jenny Dearinger

THE TOOTH SLEUTH

Dearinger

WHAT DOES BROWN BEAR WANT?

Written and Illustrated

Together, We Are FIERCE

By Jenny Dearinger

Inspired By Life Coach, Juanetta White

Juntos, Somos INVENCIBLES

Por Jenny Dearinger

Inspirado por la entrenadora de vida Juanetta White
Traducio por Genesis Tirado Bockman

www.amazon.com/author/jeniferdearinger

Made in the USA
Columbia, SC
28 November 2023

27223856R00022